# Summer

## by Gail Saunders-Smith

Content Consultant:
Lisa M. Nyberg, Ph.D.
Educator, Springfield (Oregon) Public Schools

an imprint of Capstone Press

Pebble Books are published by Capstone Press
151 Good Counsel Drive, P.O. Box 669, Mankato, Minnesota 56002
http://www.capstone-press.com

Printed in the United States of America.

2 3 4 5 6 07 06 05 04 03 02

*Library of Congress Cataloging-in-Publication Data*
Saunders-Smith, Gail.
    Summer/by Gail Saunders-Smith.
        p. cm.
    Includes bibliographical references and index.
    Summary: Simple text and photographs depict the weather, plants, animals, and activities of
summer.
    ISBN 1-56065-782-0
    1. Summer—Juvenile literature. [1. Summer.] I. Title.
    QB637.6.S28 1998
    508.2—dc21                                                                98-5041
                                                                                    CIP
                                                                                     AC

# Note to Parents and Teachers

This book describes and illustrates the changes in weather, people, plants, and
animals in summer. The close picture-text matches support early readers in
understanding the text. The text offers subtle challenges with compound and
complex sentence structures. This book also introduces early readers to
expository and content-specific vocabulary. The expository vocabulary is
defined in the Words to Know section. Early readers may need assistance in
reading some of these words. Readers also may need assistance in using the
Table of Contents, Words to Know, Read More, Internet Sites, and Index/Word
List sections of the book.

# Table of Contents

Summer is a season for playing and growing. Summer comes after spring and before autumn.

Some days are warm, and some are hot. Some days are humid. It is humid when the air feels hot and wet.

Sometimes storms happen. Storms bring heavy rain and strong wind. Some storms have lightning and thunder.

People have fun during summer. Many students are out of school. People play outside. They swim and skate.

Some people take vacations. Families may go camping or visit beaches. Some people go on picnics and cook outside.

Plants grow during summer. Some fruits and vegetables ripen. People pick strawberries and watermelons.

16

Leaves grow on trees. The leaves block the sunlight. This makes shade. Animals and people cool off in the shade.

Flowers bloom. Bees collect pollen from flowers. Pollen is a fine dust or powder that flowers make. Bees eat pollen. Hummingbirds drink nectar from flowers. Nectar is a sweet juice in flowers.

Young birds learn to fly. They learn to find food and care for themselves. Summer is a season for playing and growing.

# Words to Know

**bloom**—when a bud turns into a flower

**humid**—when the air feels hot and wet

**lightning**—a flash of bright light during a storm

**nectar**—a sweet juice inside some flowers

**picnic**—a meal that people eat outside

**pollen**—a fine dust or powder that flowers make; pollen helps flowers make seeds.

**season**—one of the four parts of a year; spring, summer, autumn, and winter

**shade**—a cool place under a tree

**storm**—bad weather that has wind, rain, thunder, and lightning

**thunder**—a loud boom or crash that follows lightning

**vacation**—a trip away from home

# Read More

**Baxter, Nicola.** *Summer.* Toppers. Chicago: Children's Press, 1996.

**Fowler, Allan.** *How Do You Know It's Summer?* Chicago: Children's Press, 1992.

**Gibbons, Gail.** *The Reasons for Seasons.* New York: Holiday House, 1995.

# Internet Sites

**Rainbow Magic Summer**
http://www.rainbow-magic.com/holidays/summer

**Signs of the Seasons**
http://www.4seasons.org.uk/projects/seasons/index.html

# Index/Word List

**Word Count: 178**
**Early-Intervention Level: 17**

**Editorial Credits**
Lois Wallentine, editor; Timothy Halldin, designer; Michelle L. Norstad, photo researcher

**Photo Credits**
International Stock/Bill Tucker, cover
KAC Productions/Kathy Adams Clark, 18
Michael Worthy, 14
Richard Hamilton Smith, 4, 8, 10
Unicorn Stock Photos/Jeff Greenberg, 1; Tom and Dee Ann McCarthy, 6;
  Dennis MacDonald, 12; Jay Foreman, 16; John L. Ebeling, 20